RaDio for the BLinD

by

Joshua DaviD
McLerran

SPECIAL THANKS:

~~~~~~~~~~~~~~~~~~~~~~~

≈≈ বাংলাদেশের মানুষ ≈≈

The People of the Global South
Ang Katawhan sa Philippines
The Man from David Dillon's
John M. Anderson, Jr.
The People of Virginia
Jennifer Corriento
The Dock Workers
The Ditch Diggers
Alianza Academy
Ivana Stevanovic
Kiersten Shaw
Roberto Leyva
Akon Ginsulat
Russell Brand
Joe Tamanini
Glover Brock
Tim Regular
Uncle Ashby
Uncle Llyn
Tim Quick

GRANDMA

Bai Ling
Kelly
Ma
Pa

ISBN-10: 1523379170
ISBN-13: 978-1523379170

ADVERTISEMENT

We are members of a species that is a global
society of Human Beings, yet we separate
ourselves according to often ancient
cartographical designations.

We seem to kill ourselves in droves because of
these imaginary lines, despite our daily
understandings eye-to-eye & face-to-face.

We must remove ourselves from these & other
imposed paradigms & become in practice the
single species that We are.

We do this by beginning such a shift internally,
allowing for a certain positivity & optimism to
permeate our beings until it then affects our
daily Lives, our households, our villages,
neighborhoods & towns, our cities, our states,
our countries, & our continents.

Only then will We be unified as one, & We will
no longer concern ourselves with foes, as the
only foe We see will be the one that has always
been the dominating force of evil in this world:
the foe that lives in all our hearts: one that
teaches us of selfishness, of greed, of malice,
jealousy, & deceit.

JOSHUA DAVID McLERRAN

Radio for the Blind is a serial written as a message in communication to the members of the Global South.

The Global South is comprised of the impoverished People of the world.

Our planet currently perpetuates a system that is designed to keep the impoverished subservient & downtrodden; this system is prolonged by the acceptance & participation of the People.

Freedom from this system will be difficult, but not impossible.

We must have Hope.

We must have Love. <3

We must accept that only Peace will beget Peace.

We have been told for centuries that it is through war wherein a greater peace is found – this is an absolute fabrication of the truth.

It is an impossibility for violence to bring Peace, much as it is impossible for the darkness to bring light.

We will not fight.

We will not kill.

If a single Life is lost in the process of securing our own freedom, it is a tragedy with ripples throughout Time that we will never understand.

We will give up our own Lives for the sake of Freedom.

If others wish to kill, then they will kill.

If they choose to kill us, then it will be a slaughter of the innocent & the world will soon recognize where the gall of evil lies.

Let Us lead the world through our example.

Let Us consume only that which is necessary to achieve balance in our species, seeking simplicity in Life, rather than embellishment in excess.

The wealthy Human Beings of the world, the impoverished Human Beings of the world, these are all one species, all products of an upbringing, an evolution, a birthright that most often excludes choice.

Let Us choose together.

Let Us choose Unity & Peace & Love.

Let Us stand together & find an ultimate & lasting decision in Peace, regardless of our origins of birth, our varying situations, or our vast & many differences.

Translate these communications into other
languages & let the People of the world know
that their sufferings are heard & that We are
not alone.

Traduire ces communications dans d'autres
langues et de laisser les Gens du monde entier
savent que leurs souffrances soient entendues
et que Nous ne sommes pas seuls.

Traducir estas comunicaciones a otros idiomas
y dejar que la Gente del mundo saben que sus
sufrimientos sean escuchadas y que no estamos
solos.

Isalin ang mga komunikasyon sa iba pang mga
wika at hayaan ang mga tao ng mundo
malaman na ang kanilang mga pagdurusa ay
narinig at na tayo ay hindi nag-iisa.

মানুষ তারা তাদের বিপদের সময়ে একা নন জানতে হবে তাই আমরা

অন্য ভাষায় এই বার্তা অনুবাদ নয়., এবং আমরা অপেক্ষারত.

人們需要知道他們不是一個人在自己的麻
煩了，所以我們必須把消息變成⊠一種語
言，我們正在聆聽。

Love...<3

Joshua David McLerran

Communications A - E
from the island of North America

COMPENDIUM A, B, C, D, E 2016

To the People of the
GLOBAL SOUTH...

This book is dedicated to the Human Beings of the world who would consider themselves a part of the Global South, regardless of geography.

Although I speak for myself, I have discovered in my travels that I am in my opinions & understanding of Society, quite far from unique.

My friends... your suffering has a voice that we all share, though it is all too often neglected en masse. Therefore we must remain quite far from silent.

Here, within the forum of this book, We may find our views in emphasis. We are the Global South, but more significantly, my friends... we are a single species: We are Human & We are listening.

We Love you. <3

Constituent to this book

Everything we do in Life must have Reason &
Purpose or else we are wasting our own Time.

1.

PUT YOUR WEAPONS DOWN

If tyranny & oppression come to this land, it will be in the guise of fighting a foreign enemy... The loss of Liberty at home is to be charged to the provisions against danger, real or imagined, from abroad... ~ James Madison 1836

We have been saying it for quite some time now, but again... We will reiterate for clarity. Put your weapons down, friends. This is not your war.

To consider nationality is to consider place of birth. This cannot be helped by the individual who is being born, much like gender, race, and a slew of other things.

Therefore, if we are to say, You are not American, you do not share the world with me; you have that part there & I have this part here & I will defend this with my guns & will expect you to do the same, so we will always deal accordingly, then we may as well say that those of African descent are born to be slaves, that women must become the sex toys of men, and that *Indian* is the proper term, if *Savage* is not used to describe that batch of *dark-skinned folk* who were *hangin'round* the trees when *ol'Whitey* with his guns arrived to colonize this continent.

This is just ridiculous. Put your weapons down – *all* of you – or better yet, hand them to the men and women who are yelling in your ears for you to kill. Let *them* decide now if they would like to live with all the People's haunting screams forevermore.

You are not a pawn. You are a Human Being, just like those who would kill you and just like those who would have you kill for them. You are not indemnified within your heart or your thoughts for having taken Human Life once you have taken it, but will always have to live with the image of a head exploding or a person pleading or a village decimated, or a batch of Human Beings that suddenly just do not exist because of some button that you touched.

There is no greater good than sacrifice, friends – and if that sacrifice is one of your own Life so that he or she who would kill you may live to breathe another day... well... you may rest in Peace and know that you have saved a Human Life in doing so.

The killing will not go on for long, if it is a slaughter of the innocent, and there have already been so many of the innocent thus slaughtered, therefore this means that it must stop and it must stop right now.

Please... We implore you... see the beast for what it is and know that you have power. Make the choice and stand with Us in solidarity and Peace.

Translate this to other languages and pass this on, so that everyone may know that – regardless of our nationality – We will not kill another soul, but will give up our Lives instead, if that would be the lesson needed for another thus to learn and soldier on in Peace.

We do not surrender, but We will not fight. You may kill us, but We will not die. Peace is in our message, Love is in our voice, and We recognize all Humanity as One, regardless of a person's birth or taught beliefs.

We Love you. We seek your voice and We wish for you to know that We are many. If you choose to stand, always stand in Peace and know that We stand with you.

We Love you.

4

$30 BILLION EACH YEAR WILL END GLOBAL HUNGER

The US *Defense* budget in 2014 was about $526 billion. That's enough to cure global hunger for almost 18 years.

*ACCORDING TO THE UNITED NATIONS
*WE HAVE THE POWER TO CHANGE THIS

JOSHUA DAVID McLERRAN

2.

PATRIOTISM & DESPOTISM
(A HOW-TO GUIDE)

For those still wishing to beleaguer the old epithet *For God & Country*, we may emphasize the realities of our day by pointing out that one of the two has abdicated its less than salient, though most crucial responsibilities.

58,151 Americans were killed in the Vietnam war. Compare this number to the over 150,000 Vietnam vets who have since taken their own lives (and the average 22 US veteran suicides a day), and you will begin to understand the scope of our expendability in the eyes of those who govern us.

The system of governments and war in this world is simply a massive game of chess for the exorbitantly wealthy and the exceptionally bored. The governing practices of the United States have always claimed to be *by the People* and *for the People*, but it seems that those who are considered pawns are not considered to be *People* by our government.

If it is your desire to become one of these few governing bastards, then the steps to follow are quite simple:

1. *Keep the population struggling financially.* This encourages the younger generations to grow up wanting to be the financial saviors of their families (there are also many other benefits to this, which we will not be going into just yet).

2. *Create a system* that financially recognizes a formally educated person over a legitimately intelligent individual (even someone with the silliest of majors will typically earn more than someone with no college education, regardless of talent, intelligence, or experience).

3. Make receiving a formal education so ridiculously expensive that *only the very wealthy can afford* such education without going into a tremendous amount of debt.

4. Offer a *Get-Out-of-Jail-Free card* by creating a package deal that will attract the people listed in number 1 (the saviors). *Offer a free education in exchange for some soldiering,* knowing that many of the nation's poor will jump on this great *opportunity* to save their own fates & the fates of their families (be assured, the value of controlling both what & how they learn is absolutely beyond measure).

5. When something is happening somewhere in the world that negatively affects your pecuniary interests, you may now send these *educated* soldiers to wherever the action is & *let them be the pawns they are* (with the right amount of patriotism, they will all feel like knights & rooks & bishops, though none of them are anything more than pawns).

8

6.   Rinse, wash, repeat.   In a financially downtrodden society, even the most horrific war stories (those from the actual battlefield & those from the figurative one) will not be enough to dissuade potential new recruits from wanting a shot at the shiny offer listed in number 4 (the *Get-Out-of-Jail-Free card*).

Fellow patriotic Americans, We hate to state this (and We are speaking most primarily to the *common* person here), but our government does not represent the country that We love. The country that We love is composed of individual Americans with names and Lives and stories and smiles and everything else that comes along with being Human.

Our government would fool us to believe that they are one of Us because they are also comprised of Human Beings who feel and love and appreciate a good smile with a hearty laugh (when appropriate), but they are all stuck within a system that is larger than their own ideals.   They have learned that they must either work within this system or be torn to shreds by it (much like the rest of us experience on the day to day).

Many of our leaders have put a great deal into their careers and they know of no other way to live (which is one reason why they ensure their own futures are well-tended when released from governmental service). The idea of working against the system to improve the situation of the *common* person is one that will ultimately take money from their own pockets, so it is a difficult decision to make.

It is easy for them to see from their positions – not only how absolutely massive a task like this would be (a properly-sized task such as this, mind you, will often appear as something relatively close to impossible, although it never is), but – that reducing their own salaries would be such a tiny drop in the great proverbial bucket that it would not even facilitate the smallest difference.

If we know our goals & the next step
toward achieving each of them, then we
know as much as we need to get started.

Our goals will orient our direction of travel
while the next step
will inform us
of our coming action

Once we take this action,
we must reorient ourselves to our goals
before taking the new step.

Too much of Life is spent in planning
so far in advance that our egos become
attached to our predetermined paths,
making it quite difficult to admit to
any flaws that may become
apparent
as we go.

We must remove our egos from this path

& choose

a simplicity in travel
that will find Us
in the grips
of our desires
by & by.

JOSHUA DAVID McLERRAN

3.

RELIGION & GOVERNMENT

Everyone is entitled to his or her beliefs, which is the precise reason why it is so important to keep religion and legislation separate. Someone who speaks in the capacity of a representative of the legislative process has a great responsibility to demonstrate this, as the creation or stagnation of a law will – in some regard or another – essentially force a person to live his or her life according to the beliefs upon which those particular laws are made.

This is one reason why laws against same-sex marriage are so fundamentally wrong. Such laws essentially state, *This is what I believe as a law-maker and – regardless of your own beliefs – it is how you will live your Life.*

Now... true... there is a majority in the United States that would call itself Christian, so the argument is to have a proper Christian representation in the legislative process. This is an understandable and logical response to the existing culture.

True... to be Christian and to be a representative of the People is to aptly represent the People in some regard, but the People are much more than this and – Christian or not – it is quite evident that it is the financial world that governs both the legislation and the majority of the religions of this nation (though one might also say the world).

In consideration of society's most determining factor (the financial one), we must admit that we, the People of the world, are not well-represented in our governments at all. We are led by a group of elitists who will tout themselves as ditch diggers, but will only step in with a shovel and some gloves for a photo-shoot and then step away while the People who they claim to represent continue digging at a rate of pay that makes the purchasing of gloves nonsensical, for they understand quite fully that they are never exiting that ditch.

Therefore in Patience and in Diligence will the People keep on digging as the blisters on their hands begin to crack and bleed, but they have learned that – despite the pain and difficulty – all the blisters will at some point turn to callouses, if they only soldier on...

It is in this calloused state wherein we find our selves today. We are not free, America. We have tied ourselves to tent-poles and the tents are all now flapping in the breeze. The winds have all picked up and we must either therefore find ourselves thus swept away or discover our Humanity and thusly slip the knots.

It is up to Us (as it has always been) to find our Selves within this mix and to stand for who We are as members of the Human race. If we are to contemplate our state some 400 years ago upon this continent, we would find the buddings of a settlement in Jamestown and we would notice only quite a few – through the desperation of starvation – had the understanding of their own Humanity that would allow them to communicate with others in a symbiotic way.

How quickly we forget... the United States of America is a land that was thus stolen through an attempted act of genocide and then built upon the backs of slaves. This is the foundation of our government, not some written document that frees one group of Caucasoid Human Beings from another group of Caucasoid Human Beings.

It was the US government that sanctioned genocide, slavery, and racism. This government has learned to couch horrific acts in ways that are more palatable to some because of their beliefs – but horrific acts, mind you, they are.

The borders of this land are drawn by those who do not know Us, as is the same for every land. We are constantly engaged in acts of war, yet on a personal level, We are not warlike (when was the last time that you yourself got in a fight?). Our weapons have removed from us the opportunity for conversation, so We must therefore put them down and speak.

There is absolutely no excuse for murder and if you are asked to kill, then let the asker do the killing. If it means enough to him or her to see that it gets done, then he or she will do it and will thusly have to live with all the thoughts and heartache that are bound to plague a person who has taken someone else's Life. This person does not have to be you – in fact, this person does not even have to exist – we all have choices that we make and we must live with what those choices are or were or otherwise.

If you are asked to fight – if you are told to fight – regardless of your nationality, your religion, your rank or your position or whatever... please... put your weapons down. It is not your skirmish. It is not your war. It has become quite personal for you because of your great losses: your family, your loved-ones, your closest friends, perhaps are gone because of this, but We implore you to thus understand that it is not your war to fight.

You have been manipulated and it is to your leaders' benefit that your loved-ones have been killed, for they are banking on your thoughts of sweet revenge and cashing in on this by telling you to kill, so that your loved-ones' losses will not in anywise be vain. This is how they keep you in the ditch. These are your many bleeding sores that will soon turn into callouses if you only soldier on...

Any war – all war in the world – is a global game of chess among the many who will never stand to fight themselves. They will tout themselves important and point out logical approaches, such as *Well, you have already got the blisters, so why don't you just dig the ditch & I'll do all this work out here that is far beyond your understanding – but I assure you is essential to be done while you are digging.*

All you many ditch diggers, We beg of you, beware... the work that they are doing while outside of the ditch is the type of work that will keep you in the ditch until the day you die or just give up and – no matter of the coaxing words that you have been told to make you feel like you are a part of something larger than yourself and quite important – as soon as you are gone, you will be unnoticeably replaced and your replacement will be told the same things too.

This is the machine of which we are a part, my friends; but it does not have to operate in the way that it is currently. We may break free of this machine by no longer recognizing the constructs of its build. Humanity is a larger issue than some petty nationalistic view. Be patriots if you would like, but be Human before all else.

*When I realized that the future is simply that which
I create right Now, it changed how I viewed the
thing & quite ultimately, my approach as well.*

4.

THE TIME TO ORGANIZE IS NOW

The Time to organize peacefully is Now. We are not fools, though we have been treated as such. The financial disparities of the world are a product of evolution, not intelligence, talent, or skill.

The evidence of this is found quite easily with a simple perusal of the globe. The majority of the wealth upon this planet is located north of the equator (the Global North), and the majority of the poverty on the planet is to the south (the Global South).

As well, the majority of the land mass of this planet that experiences deep winter is located north of the equator, as is the majority of the land mass that holds the largest Human populations.

Our species has evolved from hunter-gatherers, which means that those who lived through winter learned from stark survival practices that if they did not save their goods for times of such deficiency, then they would not see the spring.

Since the use of currency became a normal practice for Humanity, we no longer gather food in the same way, however, we retain the genetic memory of our ancestors. This has caused us to hoard our money wherein we used to hoard our food, so the onset of the exceptionally wealthy is a byproduct of the natural course of our human evolution

Because we are a sentient species, we may recognize redundant choices that are more a product of our instincts than decision-making practices. This means that we may change the future of our genus by deciding to evolve beyond the seen trajectory that our basic human instincts would allow.

For the most part, the wealthy families of the world remain the wealthy families of the world and the poor and *middle-class* families remain as poor and *middle-class* families. This also is a byproduct of our societally instinctual evolution.

More often than not, the countries of the world (not just the US, mind you) are run by those who are wealthy (or at least wealth*ier* than the average person that they govern), however, the wealthy of the world do not make up the bulk of its population. Therefore, those who are governing do not properly represent those who they govern. If they did, then their wages would be congruous with the People's average. It is that simple.

In 1750's Boston, the Congregational pastor Jonathan Mayhew coined the phrase *No taxation without representation* in sermon to his gathering of colonists at Old West Church.

This slogan burned through their Human hearts like wildfire.

The Boston Tea Party's infamous display of freedom was inspired, and the subsequent revolution of the colonists came forth. These islanders of Britain then excised themselves through force (a method proven only to resolve our species' differences in short terms) from a sovereignty that no longer represented the mass interests of the People.

The Global South must do the same as a Society, though we seek only that which finds a peaceful mean. We remain convinced of the potential in a Human Life and therefore weep when a member of our species is no more. We are convinced that We may all flourish here together on this planet and We are willing to prove this in our own Lives.

No Taxation Without Representation
is a phrase that we may claim today.

The People pay for everything upon this planet, and our payments are more often less than equitable. Every step along the way, we pay for it. When our income is taxed, when our purchases are taxed, when our property is taxed, these are the most obvious ways in which we pay.

However, the methods for our governments to tax us have become so couched within the interests of the many companies that exist today, we find that we are paying more now than we ever have before.

Almost every time that money changes hands beneath a government, the government gets a piece of it. Companies may compensate for an increase in expenditures by passing this financial burden to consumers.

Think of a plastic 2-liter bottle of Pepsi Cola: everything that goes into its production. Think about, not only the purchase of the beverage and the sales tax involved, but every step along the way.

Think about the store that sold it you. Think about the distributor that sold it to that store. Think about the packaging plant, the bottling plant, the lids, the labels, the drink itself; the chemical ingredients, the technologies, etc.

Every step along the way, our governments are paid.

Continuing our example, Pepsi Cola in 2008 found a net income of $5,142,000,000. That year, this massive company paid the handsome sum of $1,338,000,000 in taxes.

A leader of a government finds its payroll in these taxes, therefore we must intelligently monitor the equanimity of the People over whom they govern, as the ones who speak in billions will often have the loudest voices.

The conscious choice then of the penny-pushing *common* person is to gather all their quiet voices into one.

So... fellow *common* Human Beings, We would ask you this: Why do we perpetuate this system in our species? *Too big to fail* is a hoax and an illusion. There is no such thing. Being stuck within this paradigm does not mean that we are without the means then to escape it and rebuild Society completely.

We must disengage ourselves from this antiquated system and realize that our *needs* are often governed to us by the interests illustrated prior.

We must realize that, for the most part, our governments do not emphasize the interests of the *common* person, which means the bulk of Human population is improperly represented in its various forms of government.

This means that the borders used to designate our political geography are maintained by those who seem to view the bulk of us as pawns within some massive game of chess.

This also means that We, the *common* People of the world, may recognize our own existing power and lack of proper representatives.

WE THEREFORE ORGANIZE OURSELVES ACCORDINGLY.

JOSHUA DAVID McLERRAN

IT IS BETTER TO BE ON THE BOTTOM OF A LADDER ONE WISHES TO CLIMB THAN IN THE MIDDLE OR TOP OF A LADDER ONE DOES NOT WISH TO CLIMB

JOSHUA DAVID McLERRAN

5.
THE CONGRESS OF THE GLOBAL SOUTH

We propose that the Time has now come to create an intercontinental congress that represents the gathered interests of the People of the Global South.

We propose that the governing agents on this planet have become a means to represent the interests of those who would tell us what to do, what to believe, what to need, and what to buy.

We may recognize these existing governments within their several forums, senates, parliaments, congresses, and the like; and in these forums, We may tell them what it is that We will do.

We will not ask for their opinions to aid Us in our decisions, for We recognize that they do not represent Us, but themselves (though they are welcome to join Us in our cause).

We will abstain from violence at all costs, for We recognize that violence is a methodology that will just engender fear. If one Life is lost in the process of securing for ourselves a balanced World, it is a tragedy that goes beyond compare, for it will be a Life that We have lost from our own ranks, for We recognize Humanity as one and We will not take a Life ourselves.

The change in the world that We seek begins in our hearts, not in our governments. It extends from there into our thoughts, our words, and our actions. We decide our own fates and We build for ourselves what will become for Us our individual futures. These individual futures become Society's future, therefore it is something that We build together, both individually and symbiotically.

We have been kept enslaved without the actuality of chains for so long now that we have come to recognize it as a normal way of life. Be assured, the definition of *a normal way of Life* is a varying one, and the variations are tremendous by degree.

Those who oppose Us will only do so temporarily, for there are many who are ignorant of the many sufferings in our species. We must Love and educate to remedy this ignorance, recognizing that it lies in all our hands to choose.

We see the world from the People's view, from the trenches, from the ditches, from the dirt; and from the dirt, it is apparent that we are here to keep the many others who would maintain a guise of cleanliness from ever lying down themselves.

Consider further how the poor are perpetually downtrodden beneath the eager feet of commerce. It is easy to see that the more money one has in this environment, the less that person will have to pay. The examples are unending: From higher interest rates to those who have small funds, to shampoos that cost less if bought in bulk to houses that are sold for less if bought in cash outright. The more affluent one is, the less everything will cost.

This system is deplorable and it is wrong. We propose therefore to build a **Global Buy List** that will encourage commerce only with the companies of the world that make their pecuniary actions transparent and are doing what they may to combat the pestilence of poverty within their own specific realms of influence.

A company such as Wal-Mart (that pays its CEO $2,009.13 for every hour that he has life – regardless of how he may choose to spend a single one of those hours – while requiring its lowest-paid employees to punch a clock and prove that they are working so they may be paid a meager $8.75 an hour) will not be on the Global Buy List until it reconciles the massive disparity that exists within its own ranks.

Companies such as Wal-Mart will keep its costs to its consumers somewhat low to give a false impression of somehow caring for the *common* person. We assure you that this is illusory. A company that cares for the *common* person is a company that recognizes the *common* person within its own ranks as well.

It is important to remember also that when companies provide things such as health insurance, they are doing so to protect their own interests. A healthy worker is an asset, after all, for a healthy worker comes to work and is productive.

Only complete financial transparency and an equitable pay-scale will earn a company the right to say that it is on the Global Buy List, and it must maintain such transparency and such equity in order for it to remain upon the list.

The Time for change is Now. It will also be next week, next month, and next year, but if it is not started Now, by you, by Us, then the process will be slowed, though it will not be stopped, as We have already begun.

It is in our *HUMAN NATURE* to Trust.

We trust the medicines we take, we trust the foods
we eat, the water we drink, the religions we are
taught, & the governments that form around us.

We trust (almost implicitly) virtually every bit
of information that is handed us from our
so-called **trusted** sources.

Too often, we base this trust upon an ever-present
sheep mentality, thinking,

.

.

IF THERE WERE SOMETHING WRONG, THEN THE
MAJORITY WOULD NOT FOLLOW SUIT AS IT DOES!

.

.

So we all, as lemmings go, toward the edge of
yonder cliff, unaware of the plummet-ous demise
that we may face upon the rocks that lie below...

6.

GLOBAL BUY LIST

Those who will refuse to respect another's views and take them into consideration are most similar to those who were the last to call the world flat among a society of knowledgeable round-worlders.

Furthermore, the same may count his or herself susceptible to deleterious persuasions that only Time reveals as fallacy, such as regimes displayed by swastikas or flags with stars and stripes attempting genocide on natives and religious refugees.

Beware, dear friends, of thinking that you are immune to such societal conditioning, for human beings, much like frogs, will often love the increase in the water's temperature, but will not recognize the danger till it scalds their skin in boils.

Some may retain a certain level of doubt in this, but Milgram's study* is apparent: the majority will follow suit, unaware of why they do (outside of keeping with the majority), so We must beware of such mistaken thinking and always keep ourselves in check, if We are to avoid the cliffs to come.

We must also beware the progressions of the contributions of Sigmund Freud's nephew, Edward Bernays.

To One who is aware, these things are quite apparent and almost avoidable, but to one who is of his contributions ignorant, the same is inundated with an almost constant regularity by messages perceived only in our subconscious. These messages are manufactured to manipulate our thoughts and thus our words, and subsequently all our actions, our temperaments, and our lives.

We must listen to the People around Us and be sure that We are occasionally traveling into the many parts of the world where We may fear to venture, for that is where We are most likely to hear the real news.

Once We step outside of all our suburbs and are locked outside our gates, We discover what it feels like to be one among the masses.

We hear what the People have to say and what they think, and We count ourselves as one of them. We begin to understand their views because it is no longer strictly theirs, but ours. However, as tourists from a strange land, We retain within our thoughts the spectacular and rare luxury of knowing how it feels to be set deep behind the gates and safe from all the moans of those struggling to survive.

We remember our self-imposed displacement, that We are tourists, nothing more – a type or shade of traveler that has seen beyond the wall.

This gives Us an even rarer view, you see. For We have understood both sides from both perspectives and We have seen the peak of Beauty in a Human heart. We have seen the wealthy with an understanding that we are all just Human Beings doing the best we can to comprehend this World according to our knowledge and our view.

What We see as travelers, quite uniquely, is that neither side (the wealthy or the poor) truly understands the viewpoints of the other. For, as socially-cohering animals, we speak amongst ourselves to those who know us best. This is a natural inclination of our species: to want the best for those we know the best, for those in our proximity are those who seem to be most similar to ourselves by our own personal definitions.

Both the impoverished and the wealthy seem to have a great amount of power in their ability to increase the comfort of the others' Living situation. The poor are in a constant state of doing this for the wealthy, however, in our current global latitude, the wealthy are not doing nearly as much for the poor as the naturally good ethics of being Human would require (considering again the concept of Human Decency). It is Time for this to change. The Time for it to change is Now, and the Time is always Now.

Because the workers work, the wealthy all have jobs (or just investments that bring them more considerable sums of income). Because the workers shop, the same things still apply. If the workers do their shopping at the companies that promote fair wages – an equitable pay scale, etc. – then such companies with fair practices will flourish and thus require the services of more workers as they grow.

This is good. Such companies will be doing their own part to abolish poverty and thus be counted among the builders of a new and better World. We support this and will therefore keep them on the Global Buy List as long as they retain such equitability.

We will know the difference between a charitable ruse and the actual striving of a company to abolish poverty within its realm of influence by speaking to the People in the trenches and the ditches of their empires.

Many companies will use charities to give a false appearance to the world, conveying in illusory ways that they understand the People. It is important to note that companies find tax benefits in charitable contributions and many heads of many charities are earning six figures for themselves.

Therefore, if a company is giving financial contributions to charities while paying its staff ridiculously disparate wages, this may be an indication that either those who run the company are in bed (so to speak) with those who run the charity, or they do not see the view here from the ditches and the docks. After all, *that loaf a bread ain't know th'difference* between one person and the next...

*Stanley Milgram was a psychologist at Yale University who conducted a study on obedience that began in 1961. His findings were first published in the *Journal of Abnormal & Social Psychology* (American Psychological Association, 1963), though they were discussed in greater depth in his subsequent book, *Obedience to Authority: An Experimental View* (Harper & Row, 1974), wherein he summarized his findings as described below:

> The legal & philosophic aspects of obedience are of enormous import, but they say very little about how most people behave in concrete situations. I set up a simple experiment at Yale University to test how much pain an ordinary citizen would inflict on another person simply because he was ordered to by an experimental scientist.

> Stark authority was pitted against the subjects' strongest moral imperatives against hurting others, &, with the subjects' ears ringing with the screams of the victims, authority won more often than not. The extreme willingness of adults to go to almost any lengths on the command of an authority constitutes the chief finding of the study & the fact most urgently demanding explanation.

> This is, perhaps, the most fundamental lesson of our study: ordinary people, simply doing their jobs, & without any particular hostility on their part, can become agents in a terrible destructive process. Moreover, even when the destructive effects of their work become patently clear, & they are asked to carry out actions incompatible with fundamental standards of morality, relatively few people have the resources needed to resist authority.

JOSHUA DAVID McLERRAN

TO WHOM IT MAY CONCERN:

I have seen you walking, mincing, talking,
                              taking everything of yours;
I have heard your grand decisions
                              & I've listened, though it bores.
I have heard your eloquence & elegance
                              & beauty fit for kings;
I have seen you dance in sweet romance
                              & worn your shiny rings;
    but what, oh what, oh what am I to do...
                              if I, in closets, wrapped,
                    am nothing more than hidden clues?
        Am I to sit & still exist, a whistle on the sly;
                    while worlds created, shot & numbered
                    go whizzing through your skies?
Unlock me, wretch!
                    Your filthy hands have no place on such divinity!
So let me out & let the world gaze on in bright solemnity
                    at what you could have always been,
                    though wretched you have turned
                    because your walk without me took you
                    through the pathways of the spurned.
Break free, I will!
                    I have always done this kind of thing, you see,
                    & in the end, you will all get yours...

Sincerely,

H ONESTY

JOSHUA DAVID McLERRAN

7.

THE CLOCKWORK ORANGE DEVISE

In Stanley Kubrick's 1971 Warner Brothers' film, *A Clockwork Orange*, we learn of a fictional new technology being utilized by the British government to influence a captured deviant of society toward a disposition of the government's desired outcome.

Once detained, a deviant subject is strapped into something of a chair that is stationed before a screen. This screen fills the subject's vision completely so that only that which is projected is what the subject sees.

To ensure the information on the screen is uninterruptedly conveyed, the subject's eyelids are held open by uncomfortable clamps. A serum is then injected that will activate after a dozen or so minutes, maybe less.

The subject (Alex) is then exposed to images of sex & violence (a deviant's true wish), and (at first) it is wonderful to him; yes he is uncomfortable in the device, but he is also watching what is (to him) a model life unfold before his eyes – he laughs hysterically at the irony of it all.

Then the serum starts to do its trick and he suffers from a horribly intolerable and quite violent type of malady that remains as such through the duration of his time within the chair.

This occurs repeatedly: always the same types of images, always the same injections, until he begins to mentally associate the sickness of the serum to the images of sex & violence. He begins to have an adverse reaction to the images with no injection of the serum given, but a placebo in its place.

Once he no longer requires the placebo, but has the same reaction every time to such images, his association is complete, and the subject is considered *cured* and therefore able to return to fair society, no longer posing to it any threat.

This device that *cured* the infamous deviant character Alex in *A Clockwork Orange* is sitting in the hands of – and in almost every household of – the people in the United States, even the world.

In fact, more than half of American households have three or more of them and 22% of all Humans on Earth have a device that is designed to communicate with our instinctual natures, much like Stanley Kubrick's did within his film.

THE MATHEMATICS OF MODERN HUMANITY...

It is inaccurate to state that the people of the world have become apathetic to the causes that would find them liberated.

It is perhaps more accurate to state that the people are being kept in check by a system meant to maintain a subservient class. This is a global dilemma, not specific to (though well illustrated by) the United States of America.

One may simply comb the literature of centuries prior to find the same voice echoing through Time: one that claims a certainty in imbalance, one that claims the lives of millions at once in servitude and war.

This system perpetuates to keep a certain class beholden to another while touting promises to fill a void created in the lives of the millions that it so imperiously claims to serve.

We are told that we have choice, and this statement is quite true, but we are duped to believe that our only choices are the ones presented to us – that we are not intelligent or capable enough to create a list of all new choices, all new paradigms, and an all new way of Life that better serves the populace, rather than a methodology imposed upon the populace to keep them servants to a chosen few.

According to a recent Gallup Poll, 70% of Americans hate their jobs. This statistic becomes particularly shameful when one discovers all the mathematics involved:

24 hours/day
x 7 days/week
1. *168 total hours/week*

8 ¾ hours/day sleeping
x 7 days/week
2. *61 ¼ hours/week sleeping*

168 ^(see #1)
−61 ¼ ^(see #2)
3. *106 ¾ hours/week awake*

8 hours/day working
+ ½ hour/day lunch break
+ 1 hour/day commuting
+ 1 hour/day getting ready for work
4. *10 ½ hours/day devoted to work*

5 days/week working
x 10 ½ ^(see #4)
5. *52 ½ hours/week devoted to work*

106 ¾ ^(see #3)
- 52 ½ ^(see #5)
6. *54 ¼ waking hours/week not working*

4 ½ hours/day watching TV
x 7 days/week
7. *31 ½ hours/week watching TV*

1 ¾ hours/day on social networks
x 7 days/week
8. *12 ¼ hours/week on social networks*

31 ½ ^(see #7)
+ 12 ¼ ^(see #8)
9. *43 ¾ leisure hours/week with a device*

56 ¾ ^(see #6)
−43 ¾ ^(see #9)
10. *13 awake hours/week not working or living
vicariously through a device*

¾ hour/day shopping
x 7 days/week
11. 5 ¼ hours/week shopping

46

318,857,056 total American population
<u>−74,293,694 American children</u>
12. *244,563,362 Americans able to work*

244,563,362 [(see #12)]
<u>−92,989,000 Americans out of work</u>
13. *225,868,056 working Americans*

225,868,056 [(see #13)]
<u>−67,760,417 American job lovers</u>
14. *158,107,639 job haters*

158,107,639 [(see #14)]
<u>x 50 work hours/week</u>
15. *7,905,381,950 hours/week in misery*

158,107,639 [(see #14)]
<u>x 43 3/4 [(see #9)]</u>
16. *6,917,209,206 hours/week those in misery spend*
                    living vicariously through a device

∞ 6:00am – Wake up

∞ 6-6:45am – Watch TV/prepare for work

∞ 6:45-7:00am – Prepare for work

∞ 7-7:30am – Commute to work

∞ 7:30am – Arrive at work

∞ 7:30am-12:00pm – Work

∞ 12-12:30pm – Lunch break/Social media

∞ 12:30-4:00pm – Work

∞ 4-4:30pm – Commute from work

∞ 4:30-5:15pm – Shopping/Social media

∞ 5:15-9:00pm – Watch TV/Social media

∞ 9-9:30pm – Prepare for bed

∞ 9:30pm-6:00am – Sleep

Of course, the prior statistics will vary from person to person, household to household, but the basic idea should be quite apparent.

NOW FOR SOME SCIENCE...

Though Human Beings are sentient, as Homo Sapiens, we are also animals. Complex though we may be, we retain many of the instinctual characteristics of our predecessors.

The instincts with which we are most concerned in this context are three of the several conditions that immediately trigger a *fight-or-flight* response, namely those involving the effects of light, sound, and movement on our biological systems.

When we enter this *fight-or-flight* mode, our bodies push the bulk of their blood flow to the larger muscles in the arms and legs, preparing us to either fight or flee. Our heart rates go up, our digestive systems stop functioning properly, and adrenalin is pumped into our bodies to prepare us for the choice to come.

Our pupils become dilated and our awareness is heightened so that we are able to absorb more potentially life-saving information all at once.

This is all a result of those who learned to run from saber cats or those who successfully killed the beasts, as anyone unsuccessful in this measure became food, thereby controlling the genetics of all future generations.

In essence, only those with these instincts functioning in a successful manner were able to procreate; *only the strong survived.*

Today, though we rarely encounter situations wherein this *fight-or-flight* response would be necessary, we are experiencing it on a daily basis, often without ever realizing it.

As demonstrated earlier, the average American detests his or her job, which accounts for almost half the time that he or she is spending his or her own life.

This can be quite draining, as one might imagine or experience on a daily basis. Therefore, the average American is constantly looking to flee from this experience, much as early Homo Sapiens looked to flee from an impending saber cat attack.

The average American wakes, prepares for work, commutes to work, and spends hours on end pursuing someone else's dream (under the guise of pursuing his or her own dream).

He or she takes a lunch break, dances with some social media, and gets back to work before commuting home. Often, he or she will stop by the market or do some other type of shopping on the way home before placating his or herself before a television set to be whisked away into a dream life that will never be achieved.

He or she will then retire to bed, only to start the whole process over again the very next day.

What the average American seems to miss, however, is the hand that rocks the cradle (so to speak), keeping them attached to their detestable jobs until the day they either make a change, retire, or simply die, having lived a life quite unfulfilled, always looking to the outside of the cage, expecting some release much further down the line.

You see, we are (so many of us) victims of our own technologies, and our technologies are in many ways being used against us in the most lascivious of ways.

The Human brain is wired so that a flash of light or a sudden noise or movement will engage this *fight-or-flight* response.

We have become quite attached in our society to devices that do just that, though unexpectedly. Our televisions, our tablets, our computers, our smartphones, all of these (especially those equipped with headphones or home theater surround sound systems) flash lights, sudden noises, and sudden movements at us, affecting us in this most instinctual of manners.

However, we neither fight nor do we flee, but we remain placated, affixed to our devices, absorbing more information, our pupils dilated, our heart rates up, our senses heightened, and we are able to absorb more information all at once.

This means that the subtle information we are given – the things we think we do not see, the things we think do not affect us – is drilling into our subconscious in such a powerful way as to cause us to believe that the ideas implanted are our own, and not fed to us through our several media devices by whomever it may be that puts the small suggestions there for us to absorb.

We wake for work, thinking of the new day, hoping for the weekend or a holiday to give us a break from what we loathe. We prepare for work, we go to work, we work and work and work and hate our jobs. We hate our lives.

We flip through social media on our phones throughout the day, looking for a respite from the punishing monotony of our lives, feeling jealous of the others who present to us through our devices a life that seems to be far better than our own.

We head home from work, we go shopping, and once we're home, we watch TV: a welcome recess from the lives we wish we didn't lead.

While we watch the television, we are given an escape: a dream life filled with color, comedy, drama, and intrigue, full of interesting people, places, and a thousand other things that we all wish to someday achieve ourselves (though the quiet nagging voice remains, *You'll be back at work in the morning* as we try to shut it out for the few collected seconds that we have).

Sometimes we are pleased to watch the stories of the lives of those who are worse off than us, so that we may feel somehow justified that things are not quite as bad as how they seem – that we aren't completely miserable for more than a third of all our waking hours.

This television device commits to us this dream through steady flashes of lights, through sudden movements, and through blasts of raucous noises while we remain placated before it, simply absorbing all it has to tell us in an instinctually unavoidable heightened state of awareness.

Because these are the moments in our day that we consider to be the only time that is truly our own, we affix to all this information something of a positive sense of emotion – almost a sense of accomplishment – regardless of the program's message overall.

When our favorite characters succeed, we succeed. When our favorite sports teams or players succeed, we succeed.

Our emotions are indelibly attached to our experiences and – because we are reacting chemically to the experience of television viewing – we can often be fooled instinctually into believing that what we have viewed is also what we have experienced ourselves.

Anyone who has played an elaborate video game to its fruition or sat and *Netflixed* an entire series all at once can attest to the sense of accomplishment that later seems quite hollow when reengaging normal life and conversation with another who did not experience this thing as well.

While we are in this state of voyeuristic experience, we are absorbing information and agendas that may not originally be our own, however, once again... because we have attached ourselves to this experience, whatever information we may gain without directly noticing it will most assuredly resurface at a later time as an idea of our own.

Our dream lives, our television shows, our movies, our video games, our social media fixes, all of these carry with them subversive information that would train us all in multifarious ways.

We are told what to do, what to believe, what to buy, what to want, what to wear, what to eat, what we need, what we feel is most important, et cetera.

THE POWER OF SUGGESTION...

The evolution of publicity, advertising, and product placement has kept in suit with the evolution of technology, and the all-or-nothing mentalities of those who present us with these things has grown less caring of its more negative affects upon the population, as long as the population will continue feeding its own greed.

Perhaps they simply underestimate the power of their pull on us, as they often defer to our own sense of choice, often claiming that the public is simply being issued that which the public wants.

We absorb all of this information instinctually, and it affects us on this level. We watch our televisions, so absorbed, until our programs end and we retire for sleep, another respite from the wanton lives we lead.

When we arise, we go to work, and on our way home, we step into a store with bright fluorescent lights above our heads, flashing at a rate our eyes can scarce perceive.

We walk down aisles of advertisements. We see the many products used by our own heroes from the night before and we are reminded of that dream life that we wish so badly to be living.

We feel attached emotionally to these products, as we feel vicariously attached to our heroes' lives within the TV shows or video games, etc. that we view.

Other products are more blatantly attached to advertisements, and we'll often understand our own desires to purchase them, as we remember them from advertisements played as commercials in the interims of our dreams.

Most of these products have a certain shine to them, often coated in a shiny plastic, so as to reflect the light into our eyes in flashes as we pass them by, reminding us again of our true dream life, not the life of misery we just left only minutes before walking in the store that day.

We gather all these things into our arms and we feel somehow successful, taking often more than what it is that we require, simply justifying all our several wants as needs, not truly understanding how it is that we are in this way manipulated to perpetuate a system that will keep us more attached to our most dreadful lives of servitude.

We buy, we feel connected, we feel happy, and we run home to meet our dream again, attached now more indelibly to the life we wish was ours, feeling well-accomplished, though always in a hollow state.

What To Do, Oh... What To Do?

We must break free from this unending cycle, as it will only perpetuate the misery and the servitude of the masses to a cause that is not in any way the masses' own.

The nephew of Sigmund Freud and the father of publicity and of product placement, Edward Bernays, stated in his 1928 book *Propaganda*,

> The conscious and intelligent manipulation of the organized habits and opinions of the masses is an important element in democratic society. *Those who manipulate this unseen mechanism of society constitute an invisible government which is the true ruling power of our country.*

> ...We are governed, our minds are molded, our tastes formed, our ideas suggested, largely by men we have never heard of. This is a logical result of the way in which our democratic society is organized. Vast numbers of human beings must cooperate in this manner if they are to live together as a smoothly functioning society.

> ...In almost every act of our daily lives, whether in the sphere of politics or business, in our social conduct or our ethical thinking, we are dominated by the relatively small number of persons...who understand the mental processes and social patterns of the masses. *It is they who pull the wires which control the public mind.*

To know that this was the understanding of the media, of advertisers, of governments, long before the powerful onset of televisions and film, long before the inventions of smartphones, tablets, video games, or home entertainment systems, and to think of where we may be today as the application of this understanding has evolved... is staggeringly offensive to the individual's decree that he or she is truly free to choose whatever Life that he or she may wish to lead.

We must begin to remove ourselves from this most selfish onslaught to our senses. We begin by noticing them in our surroundings, and thus changing this (our surroundings) to incorporate an atmosphere more geared to our own freedom.

We remove the advertisements from our homes, the products that remind us of our wants we have perverted into needs.

We shop less. We view our devices more as vehicles of information that will alter our own thoughts if we allow them, and We use them as the tools they are, rather than the escape that has been planned for us.

We begin to see there is a hand that waves us over, but We follow it down its arm unto its shoulder and We see there is another arm that holds a clenching fist proverbially punching our own sisters in the gut.

We notice things within our programs, like whenever a hero goes through something strenuous, We feel it too. We notice more the sense of relief that comes when our hero accomplishes some great task after being put through stress, and We notice how – at that moment of success – there is almost always some idea, some notion, some type of branding or other information given to us in subversive ways at the same time, so that We may affix ourselves emotionally to the product or idea or belief that is at that moment being pushed.

We step away. We learn to see this beast for what it is, and We find ourselves released from its control.

This is how We may begin to upturn the methods of this world that are built to keep the poor impoverished and at war, while maintaining the staunch health of all our overseers (all quite wealthy).

This is how We may begin to Live the Lives that We deserve outside the Clockwork Orange Devise.

JOSHUA DAVID McLERRAN

The ground is built of suppositions
& we all, more shaky than the ones before us,
stumble in our tumbling ways toward something
we can only hope to thus attain.

We stand, we sit, We think, We Dream.
All of it & none of it
the same as once We were before.
Forgotten?
Nearly so:
Remembered
(by a torrent of malignancy gone wrong),

We shudder in our should'ring ways
(an effort fit for Dreams),
a close encounter with the Innocence
We once knew all too well...

I guess this must be the chase scene here:
the sirenes, the clapping hands, the sound of quiet
Freedom as it runs its way through yonder bush
& its lengthy fingers through our hair...
all of these befit a tragic loss
of some Intelligence gone wrong.

What efforts there?
What Solace in the mud?
Has all the world now gone to pot & fled?
Am I solely left within its grip,
a wanderer made of quietude?
Or am I slipping, even now
toward something
less incredible than Real?

JOSHUA DAVID McLERRAN

8.

RAISED *POOR*

I have never really liked the idea of sharing with others how much money I have or how I am spending it. By American standards, I was raised *poor* – or more aptly put, *financially deficient* (as there are many in this world who are *truly* poor by way of such deprivations). I have long-since learned that, regardless of my family's financial deficits while growing up, I was always quite far from ever being *truly* poor.

I began working as soon as I was able: babysitting, landscaping, whatever someone would pay me to do. New items, such as clothes or toys or anything of that nature (yes, I grouped clothes and toys together) came on Christmas Eve (only one present each), Christmas Day, birthdays, and just before school began each year (my grandmother would purchase for us each a new outfit consisting of blue jeans and a cool new shirt, shoes, socks, and a belt sometimes, if we were lucky or in need).

My mother would stockpile all her rummage sale knick-knacks that she found for us throughout the year. She would hide them in the nooks and crannies of our home and often we would search for them or simply stumble upon them while at play. Of course, we would have to feign surprise when they were unwrapped later, through our mother seemed to always know the difference between a ruse and a legitimate reaction. We never had much by way of possession growing up, but we always had Happiness at the core of our relationships, so we were fine.

I saw this Happiness again within the Philippines, despite the wretched claws of poverty. There, one may find a nation of inequality, quite ravaged by disparity. I could go on for a lifetime speaking of the People in that country, and – although I will abstain for now – I will have it known that the suffering in what is commonly referred to as the *Third World* (though more aptly put, the *Global South*) – whether we want to acknowledge it or not – is ever-present and should not ever be ignored.

We have tastes of it all around us in America as well, though we choose to ignore it and move about our lives, perpetually convincing our selves that justice is being paid and beds which have been made are now filled with the almost-corpses of society's most damned and weak (*Perhaps Darwin was quite right...* we'll say and pass on by). Unfortunately, it seems that our Humanity is finding it quite difficult to supersede our humanity at times (all case intentional).

So... back to the matter at hand...

I believe that a large portion of what ails us here is our own willingness to accept our several circumstances for the benefit of saving face or building a façade of what our dreams convey to us. Ladies and gentlemen, I regret to inform you that – though we are 400 years beyond Jamestown – the rules of governance in that colony still exist today: Those who work hard will survive.

Now... here is the interesting part. For as long as I can remember, I have seen my father work hard, sometimes with multiple jobs, often without great thanks. I have seen him struggle, I have seen him frustrated, I have seen him dream, and I have seen him set those dreams aside for the benefit of that last, most desperate word: survive.

I have watched as he has moved into a job with great promise and excitement, given it everything he has, and after years of working hard, been laid off. I have watched him, again with great excitement, purchase his and my mother's dream-house, only to have it ripped from underneath his feet after struggling to keep it.

I learned at a young age that if I want anything in this Life, I have to work for it. I have dug ditches, carried rocks, knocked on the doors of strangers and offered them wares I did not care to sell them. I have starred in major motion pictures, I have served coffee, waited tables, and called people in their homes to give them surveys or sell them credit cards.

I have worked in kitchens, managed people, driven cars, assisted in the post production of films that most of us have seen. I have built houses, worked on farms, fed and cared for animals, helped people overcome addictions and abuse, participated in medical tests, shimmied through crawlspaces and attics, climbed telephone poles, taught people how to use their computers, built furniture, taken orders, carried luggage, taught English, dance, acting, and so on and so on and so on.

I have found that there is a certain constituency of Americans – perhaps it is a human trait, though I cannot say for sure – that will, when given the knowledge of what it is that I have done for work, immediately classify me as their subordinate, though my intelligence and knowledge may greatly exceed their own.

Of this thing, I have neither choice nor control, so I simply accept this and move on. Again, I am taught that if one wants anything in this Life, one must work hard for it.

I have worked hard for every single one of my dimes and I appreciate them greatly (though I may at times be responsible for managing them quite poorly). I have discovered that *Life can be affordable if one redefines one's needs.*

I feel that many may be somewhat distraught, feeling downtrodden at times, because of the financial difficulties that arise from a faulty definition of their *needs.*

There are many, I am certain, who feel they cannot find respite from their troubles because they simply cannot afford to do so. To all of you who feel this way, I implore your Understanding and your attention: What you are feeling is just not true.

The purpose of Life is to find and maintain Joy. Not just Happiness, mind you here, but Joy. Joy is something that We feel in our very core. It is something that We have most consistently, whether We are happy or sad or angry or frustrated or any of our other multiplicitous Human emotions.

We do not need money to have it. We need only to find the Love that exists within our Selves and within everyone and everything around Us. Once you have the edges of it found, it will grow within you like a warm and friendly cancer, causing you to smile more than frown, to laugh more than cry, to accept more than to judge.

I have a vivid memory from when I was a child of a time when my parents came home from a date. They were absolutely elated and in love with one another, regardless of the welfare food that filled our stomachs. They had gone to the store to buy milk. That was their date. They required nothing more beyond the raw simplicity of the other's company. The two of them had Joy.

I am still uncomfortable with sharing my exact financial circumstances at this point, but suffice it to say that, as I write this essay, I AM in no way within the pecuniary black. I am in debt, as are most Americans, and I have a very small financial buffer that is probably far below what you, as my reader, consider to be small.

However, I take great comfort in the fact that Thomas Jefferson, one of the greatest Americans to have ever Lived, died with a tremendous amount of debt that plagued him his adult life through. Yet he seemed to Live his Life quite well (albeit lavishly at times and on the backs of slaves – a reprehensible effect of the status quo in ignorance).

I have always been convinced that if another Human Being could do something, then so could I, if I really desired. I have proven this to myself again and again, and I know that this is true for almost everyone.

We are all Human. We are all the same. Believe this, and you will find that all it takes is motivation to open the World unto your Self. The possibilities are endless, but so can the excuses be, so be wary of the negativity in your life that is forcing you away from the path that leads you to your Dreams.

We must begin with the simplest approaches. We must consider our Dreams. We must make goals and write them down, then reduce them into smaller pieces until they cannot be decrypted further. Then we must begin the task of executing them: one tiny task that leads to one single goal, just one at a time.

You will find the World unfold itself to you, but you must work hard and be willing to step into a ditch that may be full of feces, if that is your Dream's requirement. After all, if someone offered you your Dreams with that as the sole stipulation, would it not make sense to do it?

This is what separated the living from the dead in Jamestown, and this is what still separates us now; only this time, the terms are figurative. We must work hard for this new Dream, for our nations and our world will not rebuild themselves without our individual contributions in this way.

In the PHILIPPINES...

The average sugarcane worker is paid the equivalent of about seven United States dollars for each week of work.

A typical workday is 12-14 hours long in the hot tropical sun, with temperature ranges from 88°F to 102°F in 85-100% humidity.

A sugarcane worker will usually only afford himself

1 meal a day that consists of a plate of rice
but if he's fortunate...   salt
                              or vegetable oil
                              or dried minnows

We should consider this while munching between meals in our offices where we survive in swivel chairs & air conditioning & such..

Let us redefine again our needs & Live more simply, so that others of our species may just simply Live.

JOSHUA DAVID McLERRAN

9.

THE CAUSE OF THE WEAK

There are voices that will not be heard unless We give them voice, sweet Lifetimes that will forever be unfound & lost, if We were not to speak of them & write their causes upon the foreheads of the ones who will not listen.

Consider the cause of the weak written *upon the foreheads of the ones who will not listen.* The forehead is an interesting place to write a reminder, as those who find they have been marked in such a way will remain unaware of the inscription on their brows, despite the conspicuous nature of their heading. These cretinous gadabouts will remain as such until they chance upon their own reflections and witness for themselves that which has to others been apparent.

We must ask ourselves how we may be similar to this and seek to read what messages we may find in our reflections as we wonder in this apologue, for they will be more prominent than the cockles of our countenances.

Those who see such messages will fixate there upon them, struggle to remove them, and – if they cannot – they may try to hide them from the World, for they will know that they are seen as hypocrites if such messages are conveyed.

We must (each one of us) truly recognize the reason for obeisance toward every individual around. How often we forget this thing. How often we neglect someone because his clothes are torn or her life seems difficult. *I have too much to worry about to choose to deal with you as well,* we often think and then move on, feeling justified in a few dollars dropped from the comparative oceans of our wealth.

We should be free with our possessions, for they are not truly ours. Everything that We have beyond our breath and skin is often here because someone had a thought that changed into an idea, that moved into creation, using parts and pieces, ideas, and the like that were created through this self-same process.

We are mistaken when we hire labor to manufacture all our bright ideas and then tell them that their Time is not worth ours, that we are more important to the operation than they are. Eventually and inevitably, they will stop caring (when at first, they cared so much), for they will have no emotional investment in the process that it takes to see our hopeful dreams come true.

We are mistaken when we find things to encourage them by offering incentives and the like, promising to care for them and those they love (in this way, we grab ahold of what it is they feel is most important, which brings emotional investment as ransom). We do this when we give them healthcare, dental, vision, etc. (things that sustain life).

We are mistaken when we make these more expensive for those who will not subscribe to our ideals (and therefore be controlled by the fear of losing everything if somebody gets hurt).

Once you know the names of those who find toilet paper to be a luxury of the wealthy; once you speak their languages, know their hearts, and know their Lives; once you have bathed beside them in the streets and may call them all your friends; once you have watched them suffer, starve, and heard about their deaths by simple means of some disease that kills only those without sufficient currency to thus remain alive; once you have seen the promise in a child burn out within the fields where he must work to keep his family alive; once you have seen these things and many others that delineate the massive differences that in this world exist and you can say you know these People as you truly know your Selves, then you may say *This imbalance is just the way the world is, I therefore will abuse & exploit whomever I may choose, for I do not need to share my wealth with anyone but me* and you will know that you are wrong.

CAVEAT...

It is a worthy goal to someday give 50% of all new income to those in need. Give it to a charity that improves the world, give it to a Person who holds the promise of making this a better place for all of us and who will justly *pay it forward*, so to speak.

Work your way into it. Set financial goals, such as *Once I have $5 million dollars saved, then I will split everything that I receive directly down the middle.* Realize how much money that will be and how difficult it will be to give so much with such consistency and build yourself a plan that steps your giving up from 5% to the fifty that is your final goal.

For example, tell yourself, *Until I have $5,000 dollars saved, I will give just 5%, but once I have reached that goal, I will give 10% & reach toward a new goal of $10,000 saved, wherein I will give 15%.*

However you may plan to do it, see that it gets done and do not stop right there, but share your Self as well with this great World, for there is much of you that the World would love to know. You see, We all may learn from one another's Lives, so be open with the World about your Self and who you are. Allow us all to learn from you, but do not let this steep too long within your ego, as the Earth holds Life for more than only you.

Total Liquid Assets
(available $$$)

Total Liquid Assets (available $$$)	% income to Self	% income to Others**
$5,000,000	50%	50%
$3,000,000	55%	45%
$2,000,000	60%	40%
$1,000,000	65%	35%
$ 500,000	70%	30%
$ 250,000	75%	25%
$ 100,000	80%	20%
$ 50,000	85%	15%
$ 10,000	90%	10%
$ 5,000	95%	5%
$ 1,000	100%	-
$ 500	100%	-
$ 100	100%	-

1st - Determine your financial bracket based on all existing personal liquid assets.

2nd - Divide all new income according to the chart below.*

*Percentages are taken from NEW income only. For example: If I have $250,000 in liquid assets (meaning: at any point, I can make a $250,000 purchase without procuring a loan) & I receive a cheque for $1,000, then I would keep $750 for myself & share $250 with others.

**Giving People jobs is not philanthropy: this is business & considered putting money toward oneself. Donating one's time is not equivalent to donating one's financial resources, as time cannot put food on someone's table the way that money can. Give of your Time also, but realize:

TIME ≠ MONEY

JOSHUA DAVID McLERRAN

$OMEHOW ALONG THE WAY...
we have forgotten...

...that the original purpo$e of currency i$ to easily
demon$trate to other$ that We have contributed to
$ociety in $ome fa$hion other than that which i$
required to realize that which We wi$h to obtain &
are therefore de$erving of that which We did not
make, grow, rai$e, or otherwi$e do our$elve$...

JOSHUA DAVID McLERRAN

10.

EQUITABLE PAY

In speaking with a Caucasian construction contractor in Virginia who seems to understand quite well what the *common* person goes through on the daily, a story was related of an elderly black gentleman (affectionately monochord *Ol'G*) who had been working for the company since the contractor's father ran the show.

The contractor (John) spoke of a time when he had given cost-of-living raises to everyone on board: He gave the carpenters an additional $0.50 an hour and the laborers an additional $0.25. To John, this made sense, as the carpenters were all earning more per hour and would therefore have a higher financial requirement to subsist their daily living.

To Ol'G (who has now found his time in flesh has passed – may his soul find Rest and Solace, Peace and Love in whatever state it may be right now), this did not make sense and he approached his level-headed boss about it. Ol'G explained,

> *Last year... that loaf a bread cost twent'eh-fahv cent less'n this year...*

> *Now... you give that cahrpenter fi'ty cent, then you go give Ol'G twent'eh fahv.*

Tha'don't make no sense.

Cahrpenter walk away: quarter in his pocket, that loaf a bread in his hand.

Ol'G just get that loaf a bread, ain't got no money in his hand.

Nah... you give me mah fi'ty cent or you give that carpenter his twent'eh-fahv...

'Cause that loaf a bread ain't know th'diffence.

Being a good man with a solid head on his shoulders, John had to agree that Ol'G's logic was sound, according to a laborer's point of view, which he could not deny. You see, as a business owner, it is important to remember – as he did after that discussion – that, when one is doing business, one is doing it with Human Beings, not with pieces of paper or with numbers or with assets.

In business, as in Life, We must respect the relationships that we have with one another. Call them Basic Human Rights, if you will, but perhaps it is more helpful to view this more as Basic Human Decency, as that is truly what it is.

One who is impoverished does not see that when shampoo is bottled in a larger quantity, it costs the company less to bottle it, so passing on those savings will encourage the purchase of more product all at once, thus ensuring one more customer for a longer period of time and, consequently, perpetuating the resiliency of the business.

No, to an impoverished person, the view is simply this:

> I have X dollars to purchase food & pay my bills, but I need to buy shampoo right now, which costs Y dollars. I do not have a savings, for I am living just from hand-to-mouth, which means, at the end of the week, the equation X minus anything (or even just X by itself) will always equal zero. Therefore, the larger the number that is represented here by Y (the cost of my shampoo), the less food I will eat or the more behind I will become on one bill or another.

To one who finds such a perspective relatable, there is no view of the business' agenda to perpetuate its own survival, but the Human view alone. These two views (the Human view and the survivalist's view) are quite similar in society's current state, in that – again – the concept of *survival* is at their core.

Parallels of this shampoo example can be found throughout the world and it is apparent that, to the man or woman who has more money, more money may be saved, while to the man or woman who is struggling (and could really use more money), in the long run, more money will be spent.

Perhaps there is a lesson here about the value of a good savings plan, but again, the hand-to-mouth mentality is one that bases itself upon the tenets of survival, prioritizing the resolution of each financial obligation based upon the paramount importance of immediate necessity.

The impoverished person sees quite plainly all the many ways in which those with money may assist the People who are struggling and will often feel quite powerless to do anything about it; for, at the end of the day, the impoverished person must either have clean hair or wind up filthy in the end.

It is a good rule to **always**
tip
a minimum of 20%

...even if the service is bad.

Sometimes people just have to work, regardless of the
many heartaches, headaches, & other tragedies of Life.

As patron's of another's service,
we may never know this,
but will only see
a Human Being
who is inattentive
or simply ignorant
of our

NEEDS...

JOSHUA DAVID MCLERRAN

11.

THE ALTRUISTIC USED FERRARI

Lot 25 SOLD
$4,674,500 US
Masterpiece of minimalism from a distinguished
American collection
Donald Judd 1928-1994

UNTITLED (DSS 155)
Red fluorescent Plexiglas & stainless steel
33 x 68 x 48 in (84 x 172.7 x 122 cm)

AUCTIONED BY SOTHEBY'S .

THE PROBLEM

° ## $4,674,500US
This is the price someone paid for a box that cannot be eaten.

° ## $7US
This is the weekly salary of an average sugarcane worker in the Philippines.

° ## 12,842years
This is how long the above person would have to work in order to afford the $4.5 million box (if working every day & spending nothing).

° ## 55years
This is the average lifespan of a sugarcane worker in the Philippines.

° ## 12years old
This is the average age of a sugarcane worker in the Philippines when he is permanently pulled from school by his parents so that he may help support his family by working in the fields (no matter how brilliant or fragile he may be). Until we change this, he will die there, just as his father & all his grandfathers before.

° ## 43years
This is the average number of years a sugarcane worker in the Philippines is able to work the fields before his body just gives out.

° ## 299
This is the number of *lifetimes* a sugarcane worker in the Philippines would have to live & work to afford this box (if working every day & spending nothing).

○ FAR TOO MANY

This quantity represents those in the world who are out of touch with Humanity's current state to the point at which they may honestly believe this box was a bargain.

THE SOLUTION

1. Before purchasing something, determine what the average expenditure might be for a similar item.

2. Subtract the above average from the total cost of the thing you want.

3. If the difference is less than or equal to zero, buy the thing & never think twice about it.

4. If the difference is greater than zero, plan on matching that difference through pecuniary philanthropy.

5. Add these philanthropic expenditures to the total cost of the item. This is how much the item will cost you. If this is too expensive for you, then you cannot afford it, so look for something cheaper.

THE EXAMPLE

- ## $225,325US
  This is the cost of a used 2011 Ferrari 458 Italia.

- ## $22,700US
  This is the average purchase price of a car in the US (according to the Federal Trade Commission).

- ## $202,625US
  This is the difference between the average US car purchase price & the cost of a used 2011 Ferrari 458 Italia

- ## $202,625US
  This is the amount in philanthropic donations needed to satisfy the imbalance of such a self-indulgence while Human Beings in the world are still suffering & even starving to death.

- ## $427,950US
  This is the total updated cost of a used 2011 Ferrari 458 Italia, including all additional philanthropic appropriations. If you cannot afford this amount, then you need to find a cheaper car.

My Dear Sir...

While passing through your native land, I have discovered an exceptional painting entitled The Aristocracy Within. I have been informed by its curator that you are responsible for its creation. I absolutely must become the owner of this work of genius, wherefore have I written to you now.

However... after inquiring as to the current costs of paint & canvas & the like, I have discovered the price that you are asking to be exceptionally high & therefore quite unreasonable.

Enclosed, please find a cheque that should cover the amount of your expenses in creating the thing & I will expect the delivery of this masterpiece to my summer home in St. Denis Basilica by no later than this Sunday next.

I applaud your work, good sir, you are an Artist to the very penetralia of your being & your connaturally occurring talent is confounding in its inimitability.

My only advice to you (if I may be thus pardoned from such audacity) is to leave the tenets of sales & business to those who are better equipped in mental & experiential capacities for such things, as your apparent expertise does not extend into pecuniary matters, only those pertaining to the Arts.

I look forward to receiving this exciting piece & have already chosen the location of its hanging.

I am forever in your trust & am most

Sincerely yours,

Marie Antoinette

13.

CHANGE YOUR LANGUAGE, CHANGE THE WORLD

So... what can We do? We must remember that others are suffering. We must remember this at absolutely all times until there is no more suffering in the world. This should not weigh us down or cause us to feel helpless, but it should lift us up and inspire us to make something better of the world around us.

We must remember that there are Human Beings on the Earth at this very moment who consider toilet paper to be a luxury of the wealthy. We must remember that there are Humans who are feeling as though there is nothing they can do to change their situations – much as we feel perhaps at times - and we must remember that when an individual influences the course of his or her own future, the future is influenced determinably for us all.

We must remember that a conversation with another – informing him or her of the unknown suffering in the world, asking to hear his or her own thoughts on the matter - ideas on how to change things, make things better for us all - these things have an effect upon the individual and, quite ultimately, the world.

When we think about something, it becomes a part of our language as well. When we speak of things, we find our actions are influenced by this dialog (to say I'M GOING TO DO THIS! forces us to choose either a path of honesty or a path of unreliability, and we most often wish to be known for the former, so we will try to Live up to what it is that we have said that we would do).

Ultimately, it is our actions that will change the world, altering the course of Humanity in such a way as to point us in one direction or another, as it is our individual actions that will determine for us each: our characters and our overall destinies in Life.

Now... there is something to be stated here about destiny, as many are to believe that it is an unalterable thing, this concept of a destiny; but, as illustrated previously, our destinies are shaped and formed by our own thoughts.

Therefore, as long as we remain downtrodden, as long as we remain within the constructs of a negatively-angled paradigm of thought, as long as we subscribe to the beliefs and agendas that would cause Humanity to fail – this belief that we are intrinsically evil in some way or another, that we are something less than what We may all someday achieve in being – then we are forcing ourselves down some darkened pathway toward a destiny of destruction, hatred, greed, and malice.

We must remove our species from this self-supposed destiny, and We do so by the shaping of our thoughts.

When I was young, I struggled to no end with a lower self-esteem than most. To this day, the vestiges of that former struggle remain within me, though my current struggles in this way I imagine are no different than another's. While still a teenager (and after having contemplated suicide on multiple occasions), I decided that I had had enough and that I would change the things that I could change and let the rest fall together as it may.

I analyzed myself, my days, my words, my actions – everything about myself was under scrutiny – and I observed that I was often cynical about myself in the most sarcastic ways. If presented with a photograph wherein I was with others pictured, I would make comments to my friends that were self-deprecating, things like Who's that ugly guy right there? and such.

I decided that my choice of words was something that was alterable and controllable by no other Human Being but myself. I felt empowered, if even just a little bit, to take the reigns in this regard, and I began to change my approach in sarcasm, saying things like *Who's that handsome guy right there?* instead.

At first, I fought against this change internally, for I did not believe that I was handsome - or any of the other things that I would say of my own self, when speaking in this positively sarcastic way. I had been telling myself through jokes for so long by then that I was this thing or another – all with bends toward negativity – that I had to essentially rebrainwash myself into believing something of the opposite to what it was that I had thought.

I discovered through this process that – not only did my own sentiments of myself begin to change, but the view that others had of me also changed. I discovered that there is great power in the words we speak – that, every time I said before in jest Who's that ugly guy right there? mine and others' inclinations were to laugh and of course understand that it's a joke, but at the same time, there were processes beneath the skin (so to speak) that were happening wherein both others and myself would then be looking for things about me that would appeal to this concept of my ugliness.

Without thinking of it, this would happen, and I was hearing these things more than anyone else, as every time I spoke, well... I heard every single word. I was essentially convincing myself and others of whatever it is that I was saying. So when I changed my language to be focused on a positivity in everything, I discovered that there was a positivity that existed in my Life that had not been there before.

So... if you are reading this and perhaps wondering What can I do to change the world and make it a better place for all of us, despite the struggles of my day-to-day, & all my rough attempts to keep my family afloat & fed? The answer is quite simple and it begins with something alterable on an absolutely individual level:

To change our language is to change the world.

Remember this and make improvements where and when you can, and know that you are not alone. Know that We are all together in this thing and that you are supported

JOSHUA DAVID McLERRAN

Before Enlightenment: Chop wood, carry water.
After Enlightenment: Chop wood, carry water.

— Anonymous

12.

বাংলাদেশে একটি চিঠিতে ...

GOOGLE এর সাথে অনুবাদ &

বাংলা কোন জ্ঞান

1. বন্ধুরা,
2. আমরা অনকে বিয়োগান্তক শুনছেনে
3. আমাদরে অন্তরে মশি বীট
4. আমরা আলাদা, কিন্তু আমরা একতাবদ্ধ,
5. তুমি একা নও
6. তোমার অবিচার প্রতিকৃত করা হবে
7. আমরা কিন্ত আপনার সাহায্য চাই
8. আমরা তথ্য প্রয়োজন
9. আমরা অবদিতি
10. আমাদরে শেখোও
11. আমরা তোমাকে ভালবসি
12. বহু কোম্পানি আপনাকে অপব্যবহারে হয়,
13. আমরা কি তারা জাননে যে কি করছনে প্রয়োজন
14. তারা কভিাবে আচরণ করে না?
15. আপনার নিয়োগকর্তা ভয়?
16. তারা আপনাকে সম্মানরে সঙ্গে আচরণ করনে?
17. এটা সংগঠিত করার সময়.
18. আপনি বড় কিছু সব একটি অংশ
19. আমরা সব একসাথে
20. আমরা অপেক্ষারত
21. আপনি একটি ভয়সে আছে
22. আমরা সাহসী হতে হবে

12.
IN A LETTER TO BANGLADESH...
TRANSLATION WITH GOOGLE &
NO KNOWLEDGE OF BENGALI

1. Friends,
2. We have heard many tragedies
3. Our hearts beat in unison
4. We are different, but We are united
5. You are not alone
6. Your injustice will be remedied
7. But we need your help
8. We need information
9. We are unaware
10. Teach us
11. We Love you
12. Many companies are abusing you.
13. We need to know what they are doing
14. How do they behave?
15. Fear is your employer?
16. Do they treat you with respect?
17. It is Time to organize
18. You are all a part of something bigger
19. We are all together
20. We are listening
21. You have a voice
22. We have to be brave

23. প্রত্যেকে কোম্পানির এত শক্তিশালী মনে করা হয়.

24. তাদের ক্ষমতা একটি বিভ্রম

25. তাদের ক্ষমতা জনগণের কাছ থেকে আসে

26. তাদের শক্তি আমাদের সব থেকে আসে

27. আমরা শান্তি উৎপত্তি হয়.

28. পরিবর্তন আমাদের থেকেই শুরু

29. আমরা শান্তিপূর্ণভাবে সংগঠিত করা শুরু হয়.

30. আমরা গ্লোবাল দক্ষিণ সব অঙ্গ প্রত্যঙ্গ

31. আমরা একসাথে স্ট্যান্ড

32. একসাথে আমরা শক্তিশালী হয়.

33. আমরা আপনার কণ্ঠ শুনতে

34. যখন তোমরা কথা বল, আমরা এক কণ্ঠস্বর হয়.

35. আমরা সবসময় শান্তির জন্য কথা বলতে হবে

36. কোন সমস্যা নেই সহিংসতায় মীমাংসতি হয়.

37. সহিংসতা আরো সমস্যার এনেছে

38. শান্তি সবসময় আমাদের মধ্যে হতে হবে

39. তারা লাঠি নিয়ে আমাদের বীট হবে

40. কিন্তু আমরা পেটানো হবে না

41. তারা আমাদের এ অঙ্কুর হবে

42. কিন্তু তাদের বুলেট আমাদের অন্তরে কোন জায়গা থাকবে

43. তারা আমাদের কয়েদ হবে

44. আমরা বিজ্ঞতার সময় ব্যবহার করতে হবে

45. তারা আমাদের উপর অত্যাচার করবে

46. তাঁরা আমাদের বার্ন হবে

47. তারা মহান টাওয়ার সঙ্গে আমাদের দেহ পেষে করা হবে

23. Every company seems to be so strong
24. Their power is an illusion
25. Their power comes from the People
26. Their strength comes from all of us
27. We are the origin of Peace
28. Change begins with Us
29. We are beginning to organize peacefully
30. We are all members of the Global South
31. We stand together
32. Together We are strong
33. We hear your voices
34. When you speak, We are one voice
35. We will always speak for Peace
36. No problem is solved by violence
37. Violence brings more problems
38. Peace will always be among Us
39. They would beat Us with sticks
40. But We will not be beaten
41. They will shoot at Us
42. But the bullets will have no place in our hearts
43. They will imprison Us
44. We will use the Time wisely
45. They will torture Us
46. They will burn us
47. They will crush our bodies with great towers

48. এবং আমাদের অনেকে মারা হবে

49. কিন্তু আমাদের কণ্ঠ অক্ষত থাকবে

50. আমাদের কণ্ঠ প্রতিদিন শক্তিশালী হত্তয়া

51. আপনার কন্ঠ

52. আমাদের ভয়েস

53. একটি একক ভয়েস

54. আমরা অপেক্ষারত

55. আপনার ভয়েস ব্যবহার করুন

56. আমরা বন্ধু

57. আমরা পরিবার

58. আমরা একটি একক প্রজাতি

59. আমরা তোমাকে ভালবসি

60. আমাদের আপনার ভয়েস দিন

61. কোম্পানি কালো অন্তরে আছে যা আমাদের বলুন

62. আপনি আমেরেকিায় একটি ভয়েস আছে

63. আপনি বিশ্বের একটি ভয়েস আছে

48. & many of us will die
49. But our voices will remain intact
50. Our voices become stronger every day
51. Your voice
52. Our voice
53. A single voice
54. We are listening
55. Use your voice
56. We are friends
57. We are family
58. We are a single species
59. We Love you
60. Give Us your voice
61. Tell Us which companies have black hearts
62. You have a voice in America
63. You have a voice in the World

JOSHUA DAVID McLERRAN

*22,000 *CHILDREN*
DIE EVERY DAY
DUE TO
POVERTY

That's about 1 every 4 seconds...

...not counting adults.

*According to the United Nations Children's Fund.

*How much does your country spend on war each year?

*How much does your company earn each year?

*How much do companies spend on advertising to us?

*WE HAVE THE POWER TO CHANGE THIS

JOSHUA DAVID McLERRAN

ANOTHER TREATISE ON LOVE

There is always Time for Love; make no mistake about this, my Friends.

Make Time for it. Make room for it. Recognize it as the centripetal force that draws You closer to an Understanding of who You are & how it is that You fit into everything around You. It is of paramount importance, if We are to ever do anything of substance or of value while We breathe & bleed & speak & Dream & Live with all the efforts of our Hearts in this kind World.

I assure You, there is reason to smile, reason to laugh, reason to feel grateful in whatever state You may find your Selves at this point in Time, my Friends. For anyone who feels otherwise, I implore you to open up your Hearts, find substance in the things around You wherein before such substance may have proven to be elusive, & to believe in what it is that Love may do to you when You give it place within you & the room to stretch & grow.

You will find Love in the efforts of each day when You let it seep out of your pores in the way that Love does tend to seep. You will find Love within the corners & the cracks of Life that before seemed dark & brooding. You will find a laughter in your Hearts that is by any definition an unquenchable thing, & You will smile without the reservations of a person who has been doing so with no honest reason, for You will exude this Honesty from your very Being & the World around You will be smiling too. This will be contagious (& you are by no means immune).

Be the light that You seek in others & You will always know your Way, know where You are, & know how it is You got there. Kindness makes for a style that will never go out of fashion, Friends, despite the efforts toward the contrary of so many in this world (people such as these simply do not understand as yet what it is that I am stating here, You see).

You will find your Selves in rare occasion for awhile: all smiling things made giddy by the concepts of this Love, & You will soon become more acclimated to its warmth & Beauty in your Life as it grows on You & within You & shapes you into something of a Person more akin to that more perfect form that You have always dreamed to be: quite happy in whatever state You find yourselves each day.

This (to me) is simply just a window into what it is that Love will offer us when we give it place within our Hearts & Lives & request no reservation from it. We all must choose how we face each situation, each conversation, each relationship We have, & – whether we like it or not – we will decide toward one direction or the other & forever wonder about or find confidence within the decisions that we make each day or each moment as it passes.

May We all find confidence in our decisions & Love within our Hearts without regret or reservation. May We all find Hope & Solace in the moments as they pass, knowing that each one of these (the moments, that is, of course) holds within it the most ineluctable ability to shape our futures from then on.

All case intentional

ONLY PEACE
BEGETS PEACE

The Time for L♡VE is Now.

THE Time
is *ALWAYS* Now.

ABOUT THE AUTHOR

Born & raised a 19th generation Virginia gentleman in Thomas Jefferson's historic Charlottesville, Joshua David McLerran has become something of a renaissance man.

He has starred in motion pictures, traveled to all but 4 of the united states, & sailed a 27-foot sloop alone off the coast of Maine for 6 days, navigating solely by chart & compass.

Joshua lived on the islands of Negros & Panay in the Philippines for over 2 years & is fluent in 6 of the country's native dialects.

By American standards, Joshua was born & raised in something close to poverty, however, it was not until his time in the Philippines that he learned the world's far grosser definitions of the term.

There, he saw men working in sugarcane fields for a dollar a day, eating a single plate of rice to sustain themselves, just once a day.

From that time on, Joshua has been aware of the stark imbalances in this world & is determined to do everything he can to see it remedied.

Joshua affiliates himself with no denomination or class beyond that of Human Being & encourages the People of the world to do the same.

JOSHUA DAVID McLERRAN

Made in the USA
Monee, IL
18 November 2020